MALEFICAE

MALEFICAE

poems by

EMMA BOLDEN

Emma Bolden, Maleficae
© 2013 Emma Bolden

First edition, May 2013
Second printing
ISBN-13: 978-0-9823594-6-4
Printed and bound in the USA.

Cover art: Woodcut from a series of illustrations made for Francesco Maria Guazzo's 1608 *Compendium Maleficarum*. This particular woodcut accompanied Book II, Chapter V: "Of Incendiary Witchcraft."

FOR BRIGITTE WALLINGER-SCHORN AND FAMILY: *die Weite zwischen uns gibt uns die Möglichkeit einander immer in ganzer Gestalt und vor einem großen Himmel zu sehen.*

CONTENTS

THAT THEIR MEMORY MIGHT BE BLESSED, AND THEIR BONES SPRING UP
OUT OF THEIR PLACE.

-- SIRACH 46:14

THE LITURGY OF THE WORD

Maleficae dictae a Maleficiendo, seu a male de fide sentiendo.

Maleficae   meaning how by God's hand we are brought
        to belief   scattered   from sin
        by His Good Grace   our punishment
        is His warning

meaning what by God
        we are bound to believe

meaning belief in a woman

meaning belief that this woman is no longer a woman
        but beast   but creature
        granted by His Good Grace to the Devil's hands

meaning belief in this woman no longer a woman   granted to take
        in her body the Devil   his promises
        honey   nights shaking the thicket   his promises nightly
        to shake her body smooth by bramble   by rockslide   by flood

meaning   always   a woman

who wet   by the riverside
        takes into her body   the Devil's body
        she who by Good Grace   possesses the Devil nightly
        she who by Good Grace   is possessed

        she who knows him as Evil   and unlocks her knees
        she who steals for her garment   all gloss from the moon

she who brings men to bare tables   bared fists   backs
        barred by straw mats   their Faithful
        wives betrayed   she who brings

men worm-small to their wedding beds   she who lifts
          hips beneath husbands   whose wine stains
          their lips

she who with hair sun-slick even in moonfall   a woman
          of ribbons   who glistens   sent by God
          and His Good Grace   to punish   to warn the other good
          women of what good   can do

And Jesus answering, said to them: Amen, I say to you, if you shall have faith, and stagger not, not only this of the fig tree shall you do, but also if you shall say to this mountain, Take up and cast thyself into the sea, it shall be done.

-- Matthew 21:21

INCANTATION
Beginnings

After the hairline razored to reveal the scalp's skin

after the brow linden-scented until quiet and soothed

after the bared breast mirrored the moon

after the mirror wheeled forth his face on Saint Catherine's day

after Saint Ann accepted the gift of candle flame

after the palm blazed claret beneath blade

after blood smeared the tree's swollen belly of bark

after her eyes were struck shut in his field ruined by rain

after the vervain assassin swung his spiked leaf

after the garlic loosed its sharp spit in his cheeks

after the mistletoe tongued onto his broad gut

until his soured sweat rid the night of its air

until her skull purpled from pounding the wall

until her back brambled by splinter and nail

until the orchid corm made its magic of milk in her breasts

until the feet kicked her without and within

until she was a girl ungirled shackled in her own skin

until her eye widened to trace the stars' sidereal escape

until the door lost its open to become only bolt

The Witch's Apprenticeship

This is the world   you inhabit   the forest

      an ivy-ringed   frenzy   of trees

bearing leaves   and broad light   this is the world

      your skin will enter   stream-baptized and bathed

bare of village   you will first   refuse earth

      through fasting   you will unbind   the coiled vines

of your hair   you will gather   mandrake with left

      hand grasp with the right   the wise woman   who'll teach you

of its blessings   its ills   my seventh child   my daughter

      born foot-first   to this   a bronze sickle

feared by demons   a knife whose tip   licks a circle

      around ready vervain   your fingers were made

to stroke loose   the spikes shielded

      by the male fern's face   when bidden

you'll gather   artemisia   boil in clay pots well-water

      you'll pour through wanting   throats   gather rags

to cradle   what little formed of a child   these are the lips

      you'll push shut   this is the hand

that will circle her hand   the manacle   of her body broken   to be free

THE WITCH REMEMBERS
Running from the Village at Midnight

The moon a sick   face pressed

       against the sky's black   pane

shining like skin   slick in fever

       each star-   fingered grope

of grass   sent my feet

       lakeward   fevered

by the rush   of remember

       remember   dust and dust   *Thou didst promise*

to Abraham   and his seed   hanging fireside   the rabbits

       pelts matted   sacks slit and emptied

as I knew my body   would be one day be emptied   by clutch

       of root   and stem   Dianthus bursting

through whatever wound   God chooses

       to end me   in the wood's dark

I lakewashed   the skin I knew   was borrowed   I knew

       that soon   snow would start

and then the village bleeding   summer-glutted

       cow and fowl   saved   from starvation

by slaughter   red blood   flowers   a glitter

men would lick   from themselves

the taste   of rust for months

they   would feast   I

would feast   fill   my own stomach

nearly to bursting   the belly that one day would be slit

as clean as the rabbits   as God

makes each life   with his own knife inside

PALMISTRY

The stranger's   fist packed
         with sweets   his breath
basil   you'll want

        always   to be held
by him   water
        in a jug   which holds inside

itself snow   melting slow
        to wet   in his hands
his lips   promise

        nougats   honey
you will know   it never
        lasts   you will

lay   down with lions
        happy   to be prey
your men   will leave behind

        strange coins   sick crops
eyes in a child   who is not your child
        left hands   right fingers

thumbprints   they claim you
        by your father's   blade

The Witch's Apprenticeship

This is the world   you inhabit   these

       are the things   you know   lard

to massage her stomach   swollen

       honey to sweeten   the infant's

first taste   of earth   the ladder rung

       you'll give her   to hold   while squatting

this the rye   vodka

       you'll pour through her lips   these fingers will learn

how to coax her open   untie the room's knots   and free her

       of their spells   this the vinegar   to make pure

the mother   this the cardamom pod   to tempt the babe

       into air   these the questions   they'll bid you

to ask her   *who have you lain with   what man*

       have you ruined   this is your tongue still   your fist still

kneading her belly   this is the eaglestone   a good omen

       to tie to her knee   this her wail   chorused

by her child's wail   yours the right hand   to turn

       a turned skull   these the dull scissors   to slice the child's tie to her mother   the knife to shred   placenta

        to ribbon   this is the hoof   burned

to stem bleeding   this is the hemorrhage   that can't

        be contained   this is the woman   now a body

unholy   by priest forbidden   from churchyard   this is the salt

        you'll let fall   in blessing   her new-mounded grave

THE WITCH REMEMBERS
Her Early Learnings

When I learned   to speak   I learned

        to speak in   rushes   entwining

their arms   to wind   down the river   which always wanted

        to escape   its stays   I knew God

by his scrawl   on my palm

        read fir   and fire   kinder

than the neighbors   always spoke   its pop

        and hiss I learned   the snake   whispering spring

grass   and the truths   its belly gathered   the buds

        burst   as April's moon scratched   the curve

of a fingernail   pink   meaning health

        blue   sky   overhead and the lessons

of wing   of cloud   of rain   I knew

        more   than the village   its murmurs of what

I was   caught   the rat   in a jaw's lock

THE VILLAGERS SPEAK OF THEIR NEED

She will give us the world   we need   to behave   like a river

lives that lie   flat and true   as maps   she will give us

the moon in its circles   the path to   tables   stacked high

with fattened   foul and flock   bird wings

whose beatings speak to her   of what comes   of air   to us a nothing

but to her a stream   rushing   to speak   the whole world

bursting   to tell   the landscape a story   as familiar

as the story   we tell ourselves   on the flat

of our hands   to tell ourselves our hands   belong

to us   as does time   as does forever

INCANTATION
Intentions

Pray the goat keeps his teeth
    from the cabbages' skulls

pray the witch makes lame and toothless
    the thieving field-tender's child

pray April knows in her fields tied tight
    the growing ribbons of grain

pray the boats untie themselves
    to float the warriors home

pray the wife a doorway
    jambs creaking with birth

pray the drunk husband's voice
    into soft wool before nightfall

pray the trout's stomach soothed
    by your fingers' massage

pray the bull a still island
    in its sea of rough gore

pray the Virgin holds calm
    her holy tears of blood

pray the Son stays far away
    safe and satisfied in His heaven

pray that the Father
    has no left hand

THE GOAT'S SONG

Good   to eat   at noon
   the stalks   shush
     those crows   caw

       murder   in the field she
         will cry   back to them   the woman
           who feeds   down pours

           the small river   we drink
             from her hands   fall seeds
             in the field   she will show

               us her knees   she will
                   sing   as our young sing
                   the glories   of body

                   of horn   of bone

The Virgin Saves the Village from Drought

The well held   its water   beneath
   its tongue of earth   for forty days
      flames flicked   over the village

church's votive wicks   air pulsing amber
   wings   I the town virgin   I answered
      the call   though I knew no

duty   stitched into a white
   gown   the walk to the well   was bush
      and bramble   the susurration

of thorns   whispering
   red words   in the thick
      of the clearing   the village became

hands   of dress spokeshaved
   I stood   even   the light
      was an eye   doused

with water   I became   anew
   a new creature   I became stripped   of its sea
      a fish   who survived   a scaling

to stand   before the fishermen
   sanguine

THE WITCH'S VISION

By the well the women weave   their hair

      into skirts   night launders their skin

to plum   peels   their plump bodies

      curled root   and leaf inside   each woman

a tree   their husbands the axes   they tie

      to their backs   rowan   elder   the apple

tree's   arms   its hands full   of leaves   below

      blades   the women will lie   bare

stomach and breast to his   stroke   and from them

      grows   a grove of weak saplings

and in trembling   moments of air   the wolves

      circle   hold their teeth   between gums   the glint

built to tempt both   the hunter and the hand

AND I SAW A WOMAN SITTING UPON A SCARLET COLOURED BEAST, FULL OF NAMES OF BLASPHEMY, HAVING SEVEN HEADS AND TEN HORNS. AND THE WOMAN WAS CLOTHED ROUND ABOUT WITH PURPLE AND SCARLET, AND GILT WITH GOLD, AND PRECIOUS STONES AND PEARLS, HAVING A GOLDEN CUP IN HER HAND, FULL OF THE ABOMINATION AND FILTHINESS OF HER FORNICATION. AND ON HER FOREHEAD A NAME WAS WRITTEN: *A MYSTERY; BABYLON THE GREAT, THE MOTHER OF THE FORNICATIONS, AND THE ABOMINATIONS OF THE EARTH.* AND I SAW THE WOMAN DRUNK WITH THE BLOOD OF THE SAINTS, AND WITH THE BLOOD OF THE MARTYRS OF JESUS. AND I WONDERED, WHEN I HAD SEEN HER, WITH GREAT ADMIRATION.

-- REVELATIONS 17:4-6

THE WITCH SHOULD LAMENT THE WORLD

Wax men fold   their flamed
  arms over pins   or posies
    woven with night shade   a wreath

under the altar   hidden from the priest's
  eye   I thought   the world
    was a word   for me

the sallow   field wearing
  its wig of rye   emptying dark
    dreams   into the wood-

colored curve   of my ear
  malleus   pounding power   pounding
    to quiet   the body's bickering   need

and need   and need   but
  my world became   the embrace
    of flame   the sun's gold

gown a gleam   over field and   far
  I fell   from grace   to feel
    the village   unlace

my skirts   tie my right
  hand to my left hand   to the steps
    of the stake   not

yet   not yet   first
  the taste   of seared
    meat   cradling the whole

of the fire   between
  my teeth   first   the flickering
    face of the ordinary   boy I'd never quite

not seen   before
   that light   which drew upon his face
      shadows   spells   the soft

incantation   of long
   arms dancing   first
      the geography   of hands   the hushed

rustling   rumors   of pyracantha scratching
   my back   unfeeling   I
      only breathing   a world of unknowable

perfumes   calendula   candle
   wax   the red   tapers I dipped
      anointed   lit   singing a spell to create

these bushes   this moment   that
   night the hinge   our bodies made
      a door   opening

into another world   the alien
   intoxication   pink and pinker
      aster   nasturtium   poppy   fire

was a sea   in which I swam
   suspended   from his body   every
      cell's song   a singe   I

was less   flesh   than flame
   and fate   was a ring   I forged
      for my own finger   poor girl

possessed   of my own power

PALMISTRY

You will find yourself
a hum   by the hearth
the spoon   happy

to lick   soup from the pot's
broad chest   you will see
yourself a needle   aquiver

at the thrust   of thread
your hair will tie   itself with the ribbons
his hands   love only

to untie   you will lye
scour   your skirts
with stones   by the river's

thinned sides   you
will bury   the bloodied straw
for him   the pheasant

stripped   of its feathers
you   will see
your legs   spread beneath him

as wings   you will fly
to his fields   when bidden
crows cawing   of danger

of pleasure   of shame
your corset   will unlace
itself   his nails

peck   small beaks
you will gather   wild
roots   without question

you will swallow   you will pray
         the new moon   finds you bleeding
empty   of what

         he could give you   such strange
words   for shame

THE WITCH DISCOVERS HER BODY'S SECRET

In the forest the fox   dissolves   God

       the creator   caught   decreating   He

on High Holy   Unmaker   Maker

       of beggars   and bones   in my womb's

    dim zero   slow   the child grows

       from nothing   to grain   to face   the Lord

has made   another feast   for the thrushes

    for the hunger   God gave them

beaks sharp   feet blades

The Witch Is Called and Answers

The rye curled   into itself   the fields
   a thousand fists   of grain raised dry
      to accuse   the perpetual   azure

priests came   with their waters
   which their God ignored   turning on us
      forever   His disastrous

patience   His fatal blue calm   I was called
   after the thirteenth cow   died from want
      of grazing   henbane and hazel

branch   I traced a circle
   in oak woods   made
      with Him a bargain   *o God take*

from me anything   to grant   me
   this power   your power   o power
      it rained

each cloud   a gash
   of mouth   through which the sky
      screamed rain   and hail   and I

was God's answer   whirled   wet
   inside white robes   the hands
      of the village   praised me

praised my name   as it rained
   my rain   which would
      not stop   until the flood's

gray feet   kicked down
   the strongest   home

THE WITCH REMEMBERS
Her Body as Holding

Heavy   she hung   in my body   her body   turning

      leaves   dyed themselves   separate hues   as she took

shape   stretched   my skin   to become

      no longer   my body   veins surfaced

to maps   which showed only   borders

      boundaries   transgressed   the village women

crossed   their children   curled fingers

      into curses   to pay   for my cures   so many

staring   down   the bulge

      we both made   the body   built

to betray   he took   his tongue   from me   as the sky

      took   its warmth   and laid   in its place

a white body   pressed against earth   as she

      lowered herself   against   my body's base   I became

animal   pressure   pain   howl

      of wolf packs   and women   split

by the same   shriek   the same muscles

      snapped   we are all   unmade   by making

The Villagers Make Known Their Warning

In winter's wake   the men planted   a fire

in the cleared field   warmed their arms   readied

for the necessary   cruelties   of civilization   a rat

the fattest one   they found in the fields   scorched by dogwood

the long slow note   of its throat   vanished

to ash   each tooth charred   a warning to the others   *teeth*

stay in the safe   *wet pouch*   *of the mouth*   *do not*

dig the tubers   *while tender*   *never pierce*   *the young*

leaves   *at their sweetest*   for men   there is power   in this

fire   eager   as a cat   lapping   the skin off   the body

of cream   in the far   fields   around their young

the mothers huddled   transformed   to a thousand needles   quaking

The Witch Contemplates the Meaning of Time

The distance   between seed and stalk
         drooping   its weight
to harvesting   hands

         under hem   and two fingers'
journey over a thigh's   darkened skyline
         between bared back   ground

into the stone-sewn earth   and bayberries
         ground   to speed the child's
slide   to the long

         calm zero   of night   between
the blank   field and the clover
         unclenching its flat   toes to tread

the tract   between oak sapling
         and its printed stump   between
the mother's   warning   and the girl's

         palm scalded   between
the bandage   and the fat   pink worm
         of scar   between the twig

and bonfire   the soft
         bed of ash   and the blue
sleep

THE WITCH REMEMBERS
Her Child, Born a Daughter

Far the flocks gazed   geese

       sounded their traveling sounds   he said he wanted

to hold   his wife-born child's hand

       flat from birth   so no lines would web it

unfutured   slate   unscribbled   unlike

       our daughter   she   from conception   fated   fettered

to water   by stream   blessed   to witch

       whole flocks   to rest   to grant   the village

its wants   to send   their snow   a woman's body

       white   as skin between harvest   I tied her swaddling

clothes to the thorn bush   chanted for binding   prayed

       some God would take   from her the gift   that cursed us

but the wind shifted   birds beat   their air

       all seasons   all salt   the taste

of lavender   already against her   mouth   I thought

       I could stop   the earth in its greening   the girl

in her growth   I thought I could slow   to snake   be the hiss

       in her ear   to say   *never*

are you safe   with power   o never

PALMISTRY

You will be given   and taken
        you will take   small things
in return   a skein of wool

        a glimpse   of thigh
  an apple   that fits
        his palm   your tongue

will pucker   against the persimmon's
        pursed lips   an infant
will suckle   your thumb

        your breasts   never full enough
never sweet   you nurture
        the mouth's   quiet

cave   you will lie
        without   blankets
know the cold   of a broad

        back   turned
  in bed   morning
        the wide   smear

of dawn   you will
        be   a hand
full of gleam   the taste

        that sticks   to his teeth
you will be   a creature
        of hair   and thorn

the key   which turns
        in the lock   of his wounds

The Witch Curses the Man Who Betrayed Her

You are a silent   April
      holding its tongue   of grain

you are the owl's   hush
      and I   the rat

by its talons   slit   you are
      the hawk   cleaning carrion's smooth

curve   of skull   until it shines proper   polite
      without the wild   interruption

of instinct   you are   the rope
      and you   are its noose   may your wife's

breasts   become blank   may your thumb
      stroke her   sere   may her daughter

be by her own flesh   betrayed   barren
      may need   clench   her privileged

jaw   may she seek   from me
      my catmint bath   my lady's

mantle   my lettuce   to feed her
      husband lust   may our

daughter curse her   with wax slashed
      with worms pinned   with wine and with rue

may our daughter   be brought to bewitch
      by her witch   of a mother   your brutal

beauty   your gorgeous hag   your sweetest
      of all sweets   your whore

THE WITCH'S DAUGHTER SPEAKS OF HER MOTHER

My mother was a bird who flew
                              into the sun and burst   my mother was
                                                       a V of fire   my
mother flew around the fire
                        while I slept below she tapped
                                                   crosses into bread crust   my
mother was a fire
                burning itself out   when the neighbors
                                                razed their home I heard
for weeks the walled-
                    in cat   its cries small
                                        lights in the night   my mother
                                                            said it was
a distant thrush
            and then *nothing*
                        your imagination and then *the things men do*
                                                        to make their lives
comfortable my mother
                    was a fish of flame
                                    dissolved in her own river
                                                    when the cries went
out   in sleep I saw   its eyes
                            open unfleshed mouth
                                            open the bracelet
                                                        of teeth the white
jaw all
        that remained of that sound
                            my mother
                                    was a scream
                                                and smoke above
the autumn hay
            her marrow
                    the birds' yellow meal

WHO SHALL RISE UP FOR ME AGAINST THE EVILDOERS? OR WHO SHALL
STAND WITH ME AGAINST THE WORKERS OF INIQUITY?

-- PSALMS 93:16

The Liturgy of the Word

Question IV: By which Devils are the Operations of Incubus and Succubus Practised?

Consider the neighbor   who refused
       the village   refused their help
       and their hands

Consider the home   he built
       each timber unnumbered   placed
       in the exact wrong place

How the posts   carved of weak
       wood   shook even in a calmed April

How his trusses   sloped
       at too steep   an angle
       his studs bent   like beggars'
       knees

He wove his wattle   in too loose
       a lattice   daubed it with too-dry
       soil   too-old dung

Consider a woman
       she is such a house   damned
       by her very birth   to fall

Consider your neighbor's daughter
       a danger   beware the pitched secrets
       her shushing skirts keep

THE WITCH'S TESTIMONY

*Hour Seven: In Which the Witch Describeth the Transformation of Noble Men
unto Beasts*

What bared backs   curled
       hairs against my bed   what

treasures of silkworm   saliva
       what secrets pressed   by pressing

thumb   what ruby
       throats of promise   what eyes

in night   pitched blackward
       become spark   what spread

legs which loss once locked   what
       sweet   strokes   he is a hound

who licks   the lamb's blood
       from your palm   then sinks

with such sincere   intent his teeth
       into the softest   flesh he can find what   words

cold-forged rings to fit   the need spread wet
       not quite *love* but close   enough given

to take you   above me   they grunt
       the yellowed growl   of incisor

molar   canine   as the wolf who
       when I wandered   too near   bared fang

in warning   snarl   and shove   head
       against wall   against wall   then his pale

hope   spent he turns   the furred
          coat of his back   the blank   answer to any

or all of my questions   for that man
          I grew gardens   of rue   forced

through my throat's gate   the blacksmith's
          rinse   still boiling   to bring forth

the blood   he prayed for   later he cringed
          hunched on his haunches   he thrust

in his promise   then the next day at market
          he'd scent   another female   his lips

already curving   over that old empty
          howl   *love*   *love*   parting

her wide   how many   o how many   of
          you   brutal   beasts of men

THE LITURGY OF THE WORD

Question II: The Methods of Destroying and Curing Witchcraft

Consider the farmer's pet cow   favored
    from calf-hood with oats honey-sweet   ripe
    apples plucked from the tree's best
    branches   given shade and her own verdant
    circle to graze

Consider the farmer   who combed her coat soft

To her he whispered of the maid   whose skirts
    shut his eyes   against their tears and shine

To her he offered his hands   wounded by harvest
    and she gave him the gift of her tongue

Her milk blue sugar in his mouth   her lowing
    his lost mother's voice

For years he cut switches of hazel to guard her   soaked
    the sod of her stall in oil   holy
    water   her mother's milk

Consider the sixth December   whose frosts held the crops
    in their ground

Consider the heifer   still calfless   the farmer's fist heavy
    with the knife he held high

How happy   the cow   to be saved
    from her hunger   how thankful she was
    to die   for his good   her brown eyes
    glistened   then shut in grateful praise

THE WITCH'S TESTIMONY

Hour Thirteen: In Which the Witch Revealth and Describeth All Unholy
   Abuses of Holy Wives

Politely through the night   the village beauties
            raged   kicked   stones through cinders

quiet   crying in corners   those once-girls
            who found their worth   wasn't in woman

but womb   their lead powders   once used to whiten
            each wood-smooth cheek now   over-

turned   and cursed   I brought them elder
            leaves   clover   tisane

of hawthorn   far Jericho's
            roses pruned   and pinned to stained

bridal lace   at night the orchards
            pulsed   with the ghosts   of their gowns   white

silks worn   by the most fruitful figs   with the sun's
            first fingering   the brides nude

unpinned them   ran barelegged   to village
            to husband   each stem scarring

their skin with his want   and when
            ripe bellies   untouched breasts

brimmed to bursting   his hands as far as fields   they turned
            to curse me   each birth-flattened face become

a stack of sins   for him expunged   each set
            of fingers   ten more to fold   as prayers

to purge Purgatory   of his soul   and wiping
        his hands from her dripping   breasts   he took

his fingers   to glide   down the back
        of the lying-   in-maid   each red-

throated   howl of babe birthed   to hearth
        meant six   silent months for her   the untouchable

sun   behind the curved   belly of earth   they beg
        of me   to give them   their bodies

again   they beg of me   angelica   pennyroyal
        tansy   sheets bloodied   to burned   they split

their prim lips   to spit   at my threshold   when his hands
        become fists   then take themselves away

The Liturgy of the Word

Question XI: That Witches who are Midwives in Various Ways Kill the Child
Conceived in the Womb, and Procure an Abortion; or if they do not this
Offer New-born Children to Devils

Consider the cat   the queen you trust
       to keep the rats' teeth   from your crops

Consider her litter   born pitifully mewing   by God's Grace
       their lids sealed   over
       unformed eyes   their small ears
       shut   against the earth's
       crash of sound

By smell they seek   their mother   cleave
       to her   by whose warmth
       they live

She gives them suck   sweet purring   tongue
       sweeping their coats of dirt

Consider the mouth   which cleans
       and heals   wide opened
       over an unseeing face

She will devour   the smallest   the weakest

She will relish the taste   of blood
       and bone

Like this the witch   her hand bracing
       the babe's head   until the turn of her wrist   the neck snaps

THE WITCH'S TESTIMONY

Hour Thirty-Eight: In Which the Witch Responds to Queries Regarding her
Wicked Use of Herbs

Hewn by some high and wholly
        unseen   hands   the lips

of lichen   spread brown   and wet
        as a mad dog's   lyed

to white   after four morning's
        bleedings   pressed to paste

by midnight foot   step
        by step   an ounce   steeped

in milk   bidden by wreath
        of bitter   sweet nightshade   hanging

beneath the cow's hanging   rope
        of a tongue   stalled to stutter

on words stolen   by field   hands
        uncurling   loosening the knuckles

of wheat   gone too soon   to seed
        by wine the poison   delivered

by wine the poison dispelled   what potions
        what pestles   pounding   bane

by the wolf's eye   opalled
        in fire night   what fanged

wishes rustled   by straw stalks
        beneath thighs   forced from sleep

by the rich neighbor   whose joint of meat
         phlegmed   fat in slow circles   spiraled

by his hand   I cursed his lips
         for so often lowering   over the lamb's

leg severed   from harvest   by henbane
         he bade me   boil for him

tarn water   garlic   hyssop
         he who razed me   from strong and solid

beam   I found   myself made
         wordless   by the smack   and slap

of him   against hinge   unoiled   my mouth made
         screamless   by his hand's flat   my belly

kept flattened   by savine   by senna
         by horseback   by adder egg   by Ave

Maria   by mine own hand   prayer-clasped
         in the hallowed hollow   between my own breasts

The Liturgy of the Word

Question VI: Concerning Witches who copulate with Devils. Why is it that Women are chiefly addicted to Evil superstitions?

A woman alone is no woman

A woman alone is no woman but devil   the dim spirit entered through the open door
        of her sex

A woman alone is good food for the wolves

A woman alone is a vengeful child   whose hand slips again and again   to locked   larder
        to what she knows as poison   to precious
        fruit not yet ready   to leave the tree's grasp

A woman alone is the abortion waiting   inside your holy wife

A woman alone is the infant's cry   shushed to blood by the devil's knife

A woman is necessary only for making   the babes who unwatched they'd eat willingly

An unwatched woman is a waiting calamity   the spread lips of a man's early grave

An unwatched woman is not woman but Devil

A woman's lust   the trap under bright leaves

A woman's tongue   a scorpion   poison to boil a man skin to hide

A woman is the eye slit evil   the wax statue beheaded   the knife-stuck loaf

A woman is Adam's rib bent eternal   struck straight only by a man's guiding hand

THE WITCH'S TESTIMONY

Hour Twenty-Seven: In Which the Witch Describeth the Process of Copulation
with Devils in the Form of an Honourable Gentleman

Yes I imagined
    my body thrust   against the circle
                  of ice my spread
                        skirts made   yes I imagined this
                                as a lid settled over

a lake   yes I imagined
                    the depths, stilled
                      fish hung as souls
                        hang blue   in heaven confused
                            by the cold   yes his fingers

were five points of snow left
  red furrows on the white
    field of my flesh   the barn doors a mouth
                    gaping   yes I did see
                        sky fine
                        azure line laid
                            over his fields   yes the corn

husks whispered their obscene   rumors yes I kept my
                      eyes on his eyes so he would see himself
                      in me   studied the color
                      of cardamom and changing
                      weather   yes cats cried

in the corner like children
  playing or else children
    cried in the corner like cats   yes I cried
                      many times your
                      wife your wife   yes my ears held
                      the sound her skirts made

no I did not
　　struggle what would
　　　　it do any good　　　yes the cattle lowered

　　　　　　　　　　　　　themselves to the fields a drained
　　　　　　　　　　　　　　　color not quite
　　　　　　　　　　　　　　　　green his eyes　　　no his eyes

never held
　　mine he fastened
　　　them on the pine
　　　　stall against which my skull made
　　　　　the song of the pestle
　　　　　　　　　　against a seed pod　　　yes I understand the severity
　　　　　　　　　　　　　　　　　　of charges I understand
　　　　　　　　　　　　　　　　　　　of all things severity　　　no I

wished no rain by dogbone
　　by crossroads　　　by pissing
　　in riverbed　　　yes I imagined his eyes
　　　　　　　　　　　were the eyes that hide under
　　　　　　　　　　　　　our lids while we sleep　　　yes
　　　　　　　　　　　　　the wood with each
　　　　　　　　　　　　　　　thrust sent its splinters
　　　　　　　　　　　　　　　　further　　　　　yes
　　　　　　　　　　　　　　　　　　　　　　I did think

of dovetails　　　I did violet
　　　　　　　see　　　I held for a while
　　　　　　　　　　　the thought of sun heavy
　　　　　　　　　　　　as nougat　　　no his tongue was not
　　　　　　　　　　　　sweet　　　yes I ran

down the field
　　the grass
　　　crushed under my feet　　　yes I burned
　　　　　　　　　　　　　the bloodied skirts　　　yes I locked the tears
　　　　　　　　　　　　　　　　　　　at home tell me what
　　　　　　　　　　　　　　　　　　　　would they do
　　　　　　　　　　　　　　　　　　　　any good

THE LITURGY OF THE WORD

*Chapter IV: Here follows the Way whereby Witches copulate with those Devils
known as Incubi*

She will tease him with ankles   sleeves slid
        past her shoulder   she will lie
        beneath he   who appears with bright
        stockings   shoes of smooth
        leather   a swath of lace

She will give herself   to his palm
        if the coins shine inside   she will lie

with him in his marriage bed   blessed
        by His Grace

Sticking pins in his shirt sleeves   she will take the husband
        God gave you   as animals do   over grass
        over leaves   she will cast him

from your side   by knotting
        your bed clothes   she will stir
        in his soup   a potion of her own
        hair   dried snails

She will rub   mint on her belly
        to cast out   his seed   or else
        eat the womb   of a hare
        to unbind   your Holy bond
        with her child   she will turn

her bed   mountain-wise to bring forth
        a daughter   she will give
        herself at low   tide   to conceive

a mad child   she will take ergot
        of rye   she will breed
        a hoard to take you   village

She who welcomes hell inside

THE WITCH'S TESTIMONY

Hour Forty-Six: In Which the Witch Revealeth the Various Shapes that Satan
  Hath Possessed

A man of scoured grease wool   a man of mink oiled
leather   a man of swallowed flax   a man of woad

and madder trade   a man of blood absolved
by burdock   a man who bade me knot red thread

against his lovers' beds   a man who makes impossible
questions   a man who asks for heresy   the beast who rustles

shrub in hidden hunger   the beast who bears
his bloodstained teeth   the goat's teeth tearing

currants from their clusters   the veins
which lay as weary ghosts   the blade which punished

the field for giving up its grain   and the field forced
by its own nature   to answer blade with opulence

hemp   and buckwheat's flowered eyes   the slaughtered
sheep's tongue tasting sky   the brute testimony

of bared thighs   a man of steady thumb
against the grind of knife   the bell of the hare's body

hollowed   heart a sere clapper within   a man of fingers
blessed on the altar   a man of paten   pall and burse

the seed that burst from Adam's mouth   a man who barters nail and thorn
a man who makes you love him   the God who burns you

THE LITURGY OF THE WORD

*Chapter XV: How they Raise and Stir up Hailstorms and Tempests, and Cause
Lightning to Blast both Men and Beasts*

Consider the woman   you seek
      as your savior   she who you blaspheme
      as the bringer of rain

Consider that your faith   in that woman
      is faith   in a witch

Who but God   in His Good Grace
      could pry open   the clouds
      fill your mouths   with His rain

Consider the woman   we know
      as a witch

We have seen   her by crossroads
      plunge knife   in the cock's neck

We have seen   her give the Devil
      its red   raise the corpse
      in the air   through which it once flew   we have seen

her by the ash tree   dig a hole   to squat over
      we have heard   her cursed
      tongue   flap out

its curses   we have seen   her by moontide
      in the blesséd field   scratching
      her unholy thighs

Who   but woman
      the thief   snatching your grain

Who   but woman
       who God   begs us to punish
       who brings us hailstones
       who brings us harm

The Witch's Testimony

Hour Seventy-Two: In Which the Witch Describeth Her God

The rim of the wheel and the spokes held inside   the fountain
and fish   the water   the open of the fish's mouth filled with
water   the wolf's hair standing guard against rain   the rain
that slides from the wolf's slate coat   the forest marten furred
in darkness   the darkness itself   and the light lying within its
sealed lips   the delphinium forcing   its purple   skull free from
earth and the earth which forces it   to freedom   the tongue of
the pony against muzzled green and the grass which greets him
with greenness   the russet peel cradling white   flesh and the
white flesh inside cradled   the vision   sewn to the reverse of
the lid   and the lid which leads the eye to a vision   the moon
a seed pearl and the sky its woad fabric   the jug and the water
frozen in the jug's form   the limb   and the bone that stands in
its skin   the shore and the wave   which stretches its fingers
towards shore   the womb and the child quickened   inside its
wet   the lung and the breath   spreading   its sides   the fire
that warms and the fire   that frees   you of body   by burning

Neither let there be found among you any one that shall expiate his son or daughter, making them to pass through the fire: or that consulteth soothsayers, or observeth dreams and omens, neither let there be any wizard,

Nor charmer, nor any one that consulteth pythonic spirits, or fortune tellers, or that seeketh the truth from the dead. For the Lord abhorreth all these things, and for these abominations he will destroy them at thy coming.

-- Deuteronomy 18:10-12

Thou shalt not suffer a witch to live.

-- Exodus 22:18

A Public Reading of Charges

She the flail threshing clouds for rain

She the blight ridding fields of their bran

Hers the hand that shut the stars' tinny eyes

Hers the fangs that slit your pigs in their sties

Hers the blue gown lying lake on your floor

She the boat swallowed then spit in shards on the shore

She the secret abortion in woods stained with night

She who boils babes to bless her broom into flight

She who floats bloated fish bellies upstream

Hers the tongue licking the hunter's hand clean

She the mule crumpled from bones cursed to shale

She the town's secrets nacre in one ear's pale shell

THE WITCH REMEMBERS
The Village in Terms of Its Wants

How many bees   for this came

        to their deaths   how many whores

stroking pink candles   with oil

        lips lust-bloated   *kneel*

to your grandmother's   grave

        in the gloaming   knead

dough with spit   fingers

        backwards   Paternosters burn

incense and breadcrumbs   make

        *the men come   *even

the regal   well-weaned

        and rutting   women wanted

me   to read for them   signs *will he be*

        grain   of salt   or sea

winds lifted   seagulls

        circled   his leg

severed   floating a small

       boat in the sea   how

seldom I told   them what

       this world   really tells us

what flesh   tells its bone

CARMINA MALEFICARUM

The faithful fail   the devil
       more eager   for the sweet

wine appears   bitter   consider
       the evidence   of my God

he must not be   on the tongue
       of the fevered   keen

to tempt   O Lord keep
       not silence   he hath delivered

me not   the actual fact   this
       Thou hast seen   O Lord

by public threats   O Lord keep
       not silence   he breaketh

the bow   he tempts   the wicked
       more than the good   O Lord be not

far   the devil   tries all the harder
       to cutteth the spear   trouble uttered

all of my bones   shall say   Lord
       by the accused   mine eye hath seen

his desire   O my God
       his taste   deceived   O my

God I cry   in the daytime
       let them be   as chaff

but Thou   hearest
       not   the threatened   subject a witch

to examination   O
          my God   I cry   in the daytime

and in the night   season   and am not
          silent   unless   God compels

the devil   He hath also
          prepared   for him   O mine

enemies O   my God   he ordaineth
          his arrows   seduce saintly

virgins   all the more   the instruments
          of death   God I cry

they speak not peace   arrows
          against the persecutors

Thy praise all the day

Her Burning

Each flick of his tongue against my foot
                    a smoothness I didn't expect
                              fire so sudden logs stacked high by lovers
                    how bright the first tongue
licked malleolus traced tibia knee
                    I could not look at the sky
                              all was a gray through eyes blanked
                    as smoke stroked
his lips in the dark dog-warm against
                    the flat of my foot
                              became pain became not became flame
                    melting to inside of thigh
his teeth pierced to possess and I
                    gave over possession gave up body
                              gone of flesh the color flashed upwards
                    of its own accord until I
of him had tasted my mouth an open
                    gulped smoke as sweet water
                              my ears remembered the river hymn singing
                    O glory the sweet sharp
taste of feast   seared meat on his tongue
                    holding deep the history
                              of char a new self the old unfleshed
                    of flesh
flayed thighs O   I took him   inside
                    implored O
                              God on the cross that thief who You
                    saved my breath
my breath was his breath and each breath
                    a gift given taken each
                              smooth flicker licked the lids off my eyes
                    under sky's blue skin

stretched by the river frozen to mirror
                        the syrup sharp stench
                                    of foot unfooting itself
                        black blossoms
the char taste of feast when I licked he
                        rose high
                                    as my chin the fire stroked sure as a skill
                        as a hand
stroked and softly we were our own
                        melting
                                    fire a stillness I watched and the sun
                        in its separate burning
the ice threw off its blanket below
                        the hinge of my knee
                                    bent the memory kneeling
                        down to him
his teeth a secret I held
                        in the town square
                                    shadows cast flame like flame
                        wild
my breasts bit bleeding I held his child
                        hidden
                                    child daughter a wail inside my wail
                        behind the peel
beneath my flesh a hope opened
                        of mine own
                                    peeling thigh to not thigh to not foot
                        he held in his right
hand slipped itself through my skirts
                        to find
                                    not knotted rope not run not body no
                        the small
pink bundled beneath
                        red inside
                                    not mouth not wanted not water

                    not again giving
not any more mirror the rivers of water
                    not again giving up
                                        throat dissolve resolve terminus wanted
            giving up
became not snow the waters he washed
                    calendula candlewax
                                        child daughter wail hymn my disappear
            hope of water
to vanish my scent off his body
                    his hand held
                                        the twig with its starting flame

Palmistry

You   thatch
   roof   you dirt
floor   you building

   willowed   and
wandering   from its own
   foundation   you bad

seed   you crop
   thirsting   you soil
arable   and seeded

   you womb   you stomach
swollen   you hand
   too soon   sore

you kneading   you blood
   you smell   of bread
torn   you forced

   thighs   you
unforgivable   you tongue
   a bell   clapping

then stayed

The Witch's Daughter Still Lives

There were eyes   and eyes
> and *would she*
> *bewitch like her witch*
>> *of a mother   would she*
>> *be a like one*
>>> *to die*   standing

that morning
with my new mother
> I said the fire
> was an angel   I said
>> it was the story of burning

>> straw into gold and the sparks
>> were spirits   I said someone

>> was making gold   she would not

take my hand   men love
> fire and the bone it sings   men love
> the heat sweet
>> it sings   after the fire
>>> there are pieces
>>> that cannot burn   there

are no
> more eyes   there are pieces
>> of skull that once cradled
>> eyes   there is the stench

>> of hair in candle flame   she
>>> in mass once
>>> backed into a candle   and

>>> as her hair cackled
>>> they called her a curse

                                                    the bird wings

were another thing   what
they said
            was true
                  the clouds of sky   said look
                              past cloud and you're left
                                          with sky   look
                                          past sky and
                                          there's still

sky   birds fly
            left which means anger
            right which means gone   the closest
                              I came to her
                              was smoke   to breathe

                              her again in who once smelled

                                          of milkflesh
                                          and wool

as long as the sky
is a color   I'll say
            blue   she'll say
                  silver or green   and silver
                                    means a true
                                    love coming   or

                                    hail   and green
                                    in July a firstborn born

without fists   the birds
                  say danger   the birds
                              say blame   bones
                                          of their flesh undressed
                                                  men love
                                                    fire

TEXTUAL NOTES

These poems are indebted to the following sources: Heinrich Kramer and James Sprenger's *Malleus Maleficarum* ("The Hammer of Witches"), translated by the Reverend Montague Summers; James VI and I's *Dæmonologie*; Nicholas Culpeper's *The Complete Herbal*; Stephen Wilson's *The Magical Universe: Everyday Ritual and Magic in Pre-Modern Europe*; Brian Innes' *The History of Torture*; *The Witchcraft Sourcebook* and *The Witch Hunt in Early Modern Europe*, both edited by Brian P. Levack; *Witchcraft and Magic in Europe: The Period of the Witch Trials*, edited by Bengt Ankarloo and Stuart Clark.

"The Liturgy of the Word (*Question I: Whether the Belief that there are such Beings as Witches is so Essential a Part of the Catholic Faith that Obstinacy to maintain the Opposite Opinion manifestly savours of Heresy*)": "*Maleficae*" translates literally as evildoer; use of this term derives from Apuleius.

"*Maleficae dictae a maleficiendo, seu a male de fide sentiendo*" can be translated as "[They are] called Witches (evildoers) from evildoing, or from perceiving wrongly about faith." This quote appears in part one, question two of the *Malleus Maleficarum*.

"Incantation (*Beginnings*)": "Saint Catherine's day:" Saint Catherine, the patron saint of unmarried girls, was martyred on a spiked wheel.

"the vervain assassin:" Vervain, a flowering plant with spiked flowers, was used in witchcraft to cause male impotence.

"the garlic loosed," "the mistletoe licked:" Both were cures for impotence.

"the orchid corm swollen:" According to Nicholas Culpeper's *Herbal*, orchids "are hot and moist in operation, under the dominion of Dame Venus, and provoke lust exceedingly."

"The Witch's Apprenticeship": As described in Stephen Wilson's *The Magical Universe: Everyday Ritual and Magic in Pre-Modern Europe*, mandrake was considered an incredibly powerful herb and therefore would often be collected by a pair of women, so that its effects would not fall on only one woman.

Male fern spores and artemisia, or wormwood, can be used to induce abortion.

"The Witch Remembers (Running from the Village at Midnight)": "Thou didst promise // to Abraham   and his seed:" These lines are from the Requiem mass.

"The Witch's Apprenticeship": Perhaps because of their ability to give women control over their reproductive lives and because of their power in the village, midwives were connected with witchcraft. Kramer and Sprenger promote this relationship at length in the *Malleus Maleficarum*, particularly in part one, question eleven, "That Witches who are Midwives in Various Ways Kill the Child Conceived in the Womb, and Procure an Abortion;

or if they do not this Offer New-born Children to Devils," which begins "Here is set forth the truth concerning. . .horrible crimes which devils commit against infants, both in the mother's womb and afterwards. And since the devils do these things through the medium of women, and not men, this form of homicide is associated rather with women than men."

"*who have you lain with   what man // have you ruined*": According to Stephen Wilson, unmarried women were often asked who fathered their children during childbirth, since the pain was likened to the pain of torture.

"and unholy   forbidden   from churchyard": Stephen Wilson also states that women who died in childbirth were not buried in the churchyard, as their bodies were seen as unholy.

"THE VIRGIN SAVES THE TOWN FROM DROUGHT": The ritual for bringing rain is based upon a description of a common European ceremony described by Stephen Wilson in *The Magical Universe: Everyday Ritual and Magic in Pre-Modern Europe*.

"THE VILLAGERS MAKE KNOWN THEIR WARNING:" Stephen Wilson describes an early modern European ritual in which farmers would roast a rat alive as a warning to the other rats.

"THE WITCH REMEMBERS (Her Child, Born a Daughter)": "I tied her swaddling // clothes to the thorn bush": Stephen Wilson describes the practice of binding, in which a person would attempt to "bind," and therefore transfer, an illness or curse from a person to an object, often a plant.

"THE WITCH CURSES THE MAN WHO BETRAYED HER": "my catmint bath   my lady's // mantle": Culpeper states that catmint "takes away barrenness." Of lady's mantle, he writes that "[t]he distilled water drank for twenty days helps conception."

"THE WITCH'S DAUGHTER SPEAKS OF HER MOTHER": It was widely held that witchcraft was passed down from mother to daughter; therefore, if a mother was put to death for witchcraft, her daughter was also under suspicion.

"when the neighbors / razed their home I heard / for weeks the walled- / in cat:" Stephen Wilson describes a process popular in Britain and throughout Europe in which a cat was walled alive in a house to scare off vermin.

"THE LITURGY OF THE WORD": The epigraphs to the poems in "The Liturgy of the Word" series are the titles of sections of the *Malleus Maleficarum*.

"THE WITCH'S TESTIMONY (*Hour Seven: In which the Witch Describeth the Transformation of Noble Men unto Beasts*)": According to Brian Innes' *History of Torture*, a witch could not be condemned without a confession, but the confession could not be voluntary. As described in part three of *Malleus Maleficarum*, a confession was only true if driven from the heart through torture. The most common form of torture was to keep a witch awake for hours and days upon end.

"I grew gardens of rue:" According to Nicholas Culpeper, rue "provokes urine and women's courses;" it was used as an herbal abortificant.

"through the gate of throat the blacksmith's // rinse still boiling:" It was believed that swallowing the water used by blacksmiths would stimulate an abortion.

"THE WITCH'S TESTIMONY (*Hour Thirteen: In which the Witch Revealth and Describeth All Unholy Abuses of Holy Wives*):" "at night the orchards / pulsed with the ghosts of their gowns:" According to Stephen Wilson, in a common Slavonian fertility ritual, a woman would pin her chemise to a fertile tree, often a fig tree, through the night and then put it on her own body in the morning.

"each set // of fingers ten more to fold themselves as prayers:" In early modern Europe, children were expected to pray and say masses to expedite their parents' souls' journey through Purgatory; therefore, the more children one had, the less time one's soul would spend in Purgatory.

"another six // months shuttered:" After giving birth, a woman was to stay inside for six months, to avoid risk of bewitching.

"THE WITCH'S TESTIMONY (*Hour Thirty Eight: In which the Witch Responds to Queries Regarding her Wicked Use of Herbs)*": "severed from harvest by henbane": Henbane is a poisonous plant; Culpeper warns that "[t]his herb must never be taken inwardly."

"he bade me boil for him // tarn water garlic hyssop": Culpeper writes of garlic's power to purge poison from the body: "[i]t has a special quality to discuss inconveniences, coming by corrupt agues or mineral vapours; by drinking corrupt and stinking waters; or by taking Wolf'sbane, Henbane, Hemlock or other poisonous and dangerous herbs." Hyssop, Culpeper writers, is "[a] most violent purgative."

"THE LITURGY OF THE WORD (*Question VI: Concerning Witches who copulate with Devils. Why is it that Women are chiefly addicted to Evil superstitions?)*": "A woman is Adam's rib bent eternal": Kramer and Sprenger record the following belief in their *Malleus Maleficarum*: "And it should be noted that there was a defect in the formation of the first woman, since she was formed from a bent rib, that is, a rib of the breast, which is bent as it were in a contrary direction to a man. And since through this defect she is an imperfect animal, she always deceives."

"THE LITURGY OF THE WORD (*Chapter IV: Here follows the Way whereby Witches copulate with those Devils known as Incubi)*": "her bed mountain-wise to bring forth / a daughter she will give/ herself at low tide": According to Stephen Wilson, it was widely believed that such practices would lead to the conception of a girl, who would be seen as a curse, as sons were desired.

to conceive // a mad child   she will take ergot /   of rye": Stephen Wilson also describes the belief that a mother's mental state at the moment of conception would influence the personality of the child.

"THE WITCH'S TESTIMONY (*Hour Forty Six: In which the Witch Revealeth the Various Shapes that Satan Hath Possessed*):" "a man of blood absolved / by burdock": Burdock works to purify the blood.

"a man of paten   pall and burse": The paten is a small plate used to hold the host in the Eucharist. The pall is a piece of cloth used to cover the chalice. The burse serves as a receptacle in which the corporal, the cloth upon which the chalice and paten are placed, is carried from the altar.

"the seed that burst / from Adam's mouth:" In early modern Europe, popular thought held that the tree upon which Christ was crucified sprung from Adam's mouth.

"*CARMINA MALEFICARUM*:" The text of this poem is derived from the Psalms and *Malleus Maleficarum*.

ACKNOWLEDGEMENTS

My thanks to the editors of following journals, in which poems from *Maleficae*, or versions of them, originally appeared: *American Poetry Journal, Campbell Corner Poetry Prize, Cincinnati Review, Copper Nickel, The Cortland Review, Country Dog Review, Feminist Studies, The Greensboro Review, Guernica, Indiana Review, James Dickey Review, The Journal, Linebreak, Memorious, Prairie Schooner, PIF Magazine, Red Mountain Review, Redivider, Sawbuck, Southern Humanities Review, Tapestry,* and *Whiskey Island.*

Much gratitude to the faculty and staff of the Alabama School of Fine Arts, Auburn University, Georgetown College, and Georgia Southern University. Thanks to Robyn Morgan, Father Louie Skipper, Christian Peet, Nancy Noe, Juliet Rumble, Andrew Wohrley, Holly Barbaccia, Diane Arnson Svarlien, Jennifer Shaiman, George Cusack, Chantel Acevedo, Ross White, Kate Knapp Johnson, Thomas Lux, Sarah Messer, Mark Cox, Diann Blakely, Hannah Dela Cruz Abrams, Gina Putthoff, and Kristin Czarnecki. Gratitude, then more gratitude, and love, then more love, always, to my parents, who've held me up every single step of the way.

Finally, to the witches: *Requiem æternam dona eis, Domine, et lux perpetua luceat eis.*

ABOUT THE AUTHOR

Emma Bolden was born and raised in Alabama. She is the author of three chapbooks of poetry: *How to Recognize a Lady,* (part of *Edge by Edge,* the third in Toadlily Press' Quartet Series); *The Mariner's Wife* (Finishing Line Press); and *The Sad Epistles* (Dancing Girl Press). Her manuscripts have been semi-finalists for the Crab Orchard Review Poetry Series' First Book Prize, the Perugia Press Book Prize, the Brittingham and Felix Pollak Prizes in Poetry, and the Blue Lynx Prize for Poetry, as well as a finalist for the Cleveland State University Poetry Center's First Book Prize. She received a BLA from Sarah Lawrence College and an MFA from the University of North Carolina Wilmington. She is an assistant professor of Creative Writing at Georgia Southern University and blogs at *A Century of Nerve* (emmabolden.com).

AVAILABLE FROM GENPOP BOOKS

Judith Baumel, *The Kangaroo Girl*

Emma Bolden, *Maleficae*

Michael Klein, *then, we were still living*

John Philpin, *Bad Dog*

Julianna Spallholz, *The State of Kansas*

Alan Semerdjian, *In the Architecture of Bone*

www.genpopbooks.com